GW00838456

First Published 1989
Reprinted 1990, 1992
Learning Development Aids
Duke Street, Wisbech, Cambs PE13 2AE

© University of Reading

ISBN 0 905 114 70 1

Designed by C.M.Z. Quantum Graphics

Typesetting by Chameleon Typesetting

Printed by Ebenezer Baylis & Son Ltd, Worcester

WORD
for
WORD

The Top 2,000 Words Used By 7 and 8 Year Olds

Dee Reid

Part-Time Research Assistant
The Reading and Language Information Centre
University of Reading

Contents

Foreword

The Reading and Language Information Centre in the University of Reading would like to thank Learning Development Aids for funding this research project and for publishing it.

For many years it has been recognised that the existing vocabulary lists were out of date and certainly the new list confirms this.

By publishing Word For Word we have presented new information about the words that children in the 80's use in their writing. The Research Team has offered some basic observations and comparisons, but acknowledge the fact that such analysis only scratches the surface. Many more books could be filled with detailed examination of all the fascinating insights that these lists of words offer.

Like many research undertakings this proved to be much more complicated than was initially envisaged. Our thanks are due to Dr Bridie Raban for generously passing on her extensive knowledge of the capabilities of the main frame computer in the University.

It was a very long and tedious task to transfer all the original data on to disc and the Centre is indepted to Mary Buck who did this with interest and enthusiasm.

It is felt certain that teachers, researchers and publishers will find Word For Word extremely useful.

Betty Root
Tutor-in-Charge
Reading and Language Information Centre

The purpose of the research project run by the Reading and Language Centre of the University of Reading was to create an up-to-date vocabulary list of the words most frequently used by children aged 7-8 years.

A History Of Word Lists

In Australia in the 1930's, Schonell compiled his 'List of Everyday Words for English Children'. The data for this list was derived from a study compiled by Ernest Horn in America in 1926. Horn analysed 10,000 words most commonly used in writing by *adults*. Schonell contrasted this list with a list compiled by Thorndike (USA) in 1921. He also surveyed examples of children's written English to reach a final 3,200 words as a spelling vocabulary for children aged 7-13 years.

Arvidson, in New Zealand, compiled the data for his 'Spelling List' based on American research in the early 1950's. He invited teachers to comment upon the New York list and to make any deletions or additions considered necessary. He also cross-referenced this with 'word-counts' made from children's writing in several Wellington schools. In this way, the 2,700 words of the New Zealand list were gradually selected.

In 1957 Burroughs investigated the spoken vocabulary of 330 children in schools in the Midlands. The present project has not drawn any close comparisons with this study because it analysed a *spoken* rather than a *written* vocabulary.

It is significant that several of the above vocabulary lists were based on research conducted outside Britain, and yet were assumed to be suitable to be adopted by British schools.

To remedy this situation an 'Infant Vocabulary Survey' was conducted in Leicestershire in 1963 by Edwards and Gibbon to determine the words children use in their writing. Five to seven-year old children were the focus of this study. The written work of 2,120 children was used. The survey concentrated upon comparisons with the words lists achieved and the vocabulary of scheme readers notably 'Janet and John' and 'Happy Venture'. The researchers concluded that publishers should ensure that the vocabulary of their scheme readers should be revised to suit the words children choose to use.

No. of schools replying		
Nov '86	19 Rural 15 Urban	34
Feb '87	21 Rural 31 Urban	52
March '87	19 Rural 19 Urban	38
May '87	24 Rural 16 Urban	40
June '87	19 Rural 23 Urban	42
		206

Response to the Survey

In total, 979 scripts from 7-year olds were examined and 1,627 scripts from 8-year olds were examined.

Total 2,606

The research project that finally created the word lists contained in Word For Word concentrated upon the age range 7-8 years. It differed significantly to the ethos underlying the previous research in that it was not devised simply to determine suitable word lists for spelling, or to advise on vocabulary for reading scheme books. The overriding purpose of the research was to discover subjects of interest to children and the levels of thinking that children demonstrate through the written medium.

How the research was carried out

A random sample of schools in Great Britain was drawn from the list of schools which are members of the Reading and Language Information Centre. 3,600 schools are registered and from that number 500 schools were randomly selected. This sampling was evenly balanced between urban and rural schools.

The data was collected in five batches of 100 schools each in November 1986, January, March, May and June 1987. The schools ranged in size from those with under 50 on the roll to large urban schools with over 400 pupils.

Each school was asked to provide 10 samples of spontaneous writing from each of the following age groups: 7-8 years; 8-9 years; 9-10 years. For the purposes of this study only the responses from the first two categories were analysed. Teachers were directed to provide examples of uncorrected spontaneous writing from across the ability range and to include a variety of purposes of writing — imaginative, factual, descriptive etc.

There was a 41% response from the schools over the year and this realized 979 pieces of writing from 7-year olds and 1,627 pieces of writing from 8-year olds. In total 2,606 scripts were examined.

In some instances, schools returned less than the full complement of 10 scripts per age group. In some cases this was because the school did not have ten children in that age group. Also, as the survey continued, there was a decrease in the number of scripts received from 7-year olds. This was because as the school year progressed there were fewer 7-year olds in Junior classes and, for schools which have separate sites for Juniors and Infants, it was too difficult to include in the sample the growing number of 7-year olds in the Infant school.

THE WORD LISTS

The Top 2,000 Words Used By 7-Year Olds In Their Writing

look . could ✓people ✓big ✓down
✓see your ✓their ✓dad from .

Word	Frequency	Rank	Word	Frequency	Rank
and	6204	1	but	551	27
the	6079	2	me	543	28
a	3366	3	up	518	29
I	3195	4	for	508	30
to	2650	5	with	494	31
was	2153	6	day	489	32
it	1689	7	out	457	33
he	1569	8	that	457	34
we	1453	9	some	456	35
in	1438	10	go	444	36
went	1352	11	his	434	37
my	1246	12	have	433	38
they	1065	13	came	423	39
then	1050	14	were	408	40
on	1049	15	saw	395	41
of	1038	16	all	378	42
said	863	17	at	371	43
had	831	18	her	371	44
is	688	19	home	349	45
got	670	20	not	325	46
she	656	21	like	323	47
when	646	22	very	302	48
you	611	23	are	294	49
so	607	24	get	290	50
there	604	25	him	285	51
one	581	26	down	282	52

back	279	53	dog	170	80
mum	279	54	off	170	81
them	279	55	(see)	169	82
because	273	56	(people)	168	83
put	244	57	two	168	84
into	240	58	come	166	85
will	237	59	our	166	86
did	236	60	school	166	87
man	236	61	once	165	88
little	233	62	if	159	89
time	228	63	door	156	90
big	226	64	ran	155	91
house	222	65	no	152	92
called	209	66	next	151	93
would	205	67	took	150	94
dad	200	68	good	148	95
their	192	69	an	147	96
has	188	70	about	143	97
can	183	71	night	143	98
be	179	72	name	142	99
could	179	73	made	140	100
going	178	74	tree	136	101
bed	176	75	over	135	102
do	176	76	again	134	103
after	175	77	yes	134	104
what	172	78	from	133	105
as	170	79	us	130	106

TIB WK3

TIB WK4

TIB WK5.

TIB WK 6

2 3 4 5 6 7 8

6

9	boy	129	107	who	87	134	
10	away	128	108	way	86	135	
T2A WK1	this	124	109	dragon	84	136	
2	old	122	110	red	84	137	
3	found	120	111	round	84	138	
4	lived	119	112	mummy	83	139	
5	play	111	113	well T2SWK1.	83	140	
6	girl	110	114	where	83	141	
7	told	108	115	gave	82	142	
8	fell	105	116	lots	82	143	
9	morning	105	117	want	82	144	
10	started	102	118	friend	81	145	
T2B WK3 (1)	other	101	119	children	80	146	
2	water	101	120	make	80	147	
3	your	101	121	tea	80	148	
4	am	100	122	through	80	149	
5	first	100	123	car T3AWK1.	79	150	
6	just	100	124	another	78	151	
7	now	100	125	heard	78	152	
8	long	98	126	king	78	153	
9	looked	97	127	more	78	154	
10	too	97	128	playing	78	155	
10	thought	94	129	fire	77	156	
2A WK4	by	91	130	white	77	157	
	walk	91	131	garden	76	158	
	cat	90	132	nice	76	159	
	upon	89	133	friends	75	160	

don't	74	161	opened	62	188
oh	74	162	park	62	189
take	74	163	giant	61	190
hair	73	164	gone	61	191
three	73	165	room	61	192
help	72	166	sister	61	193
here	72	167	asked	60	194
how	72	168	blue	60	195
played	72	169	or	60	196
eyes	71	170	outside	60	197
shop	70	171	bad	59	198
balloon	69	172	brother	59	199
black	69	173	sleep	59	200
Christmas	69	174	cave	58	201
look	69	175	trees	58	202
eat	68	176	woke	58	203
things	68	177	never	57	204
witch	68	178	tried	57	205
something	66	179	best	56	206
know	65	180	bit	56	207
think	65	181	dark	56	208
give	64	182	end	56	209
story	63	183	always	55	210
walked	63	184	baby	55	211
castle	62	185	boat	55	212
didn't	62	186	lot	55	213
food	62	187	wood	55	214

8

daddy	54	215		sea	47	242
green	54	216		thing	47	243
it's	54	217		gold	46	244
lady	54	218		hole	46	245
soon	54	219		walking	46	246
fair	53	220		ever	45	247
its	53	221		let	45	248
men	53	222		lost	45	249
Mr	53	223		mother	45	250
only	53	224		often	45	251
snowman	52	225		sometimes	45	252
suddenly	52	226		cold	44	253
wind	52	227		fish	44	254
dinner	51	228		magic	44	255
find	51	229		right	44	256
sad	51	230		still	44	257
run	50	231		zoo	44	258
turned	50	232		goes	43	259
clothes	49	233		money	43	260
football	49	234		tell	43	261
top	49	235		window	43	262
wanted	49	236		beanstalk	42	263
why	49	237		father	42	264
sunflower	48	238		I'm	42	265
around	47	239		road	42	266
bird	47	240		side	42	267
head	47	241		stopped	42	268

work	42	269	finished	37	296
flew	41	270	liked	37	297
jumped	41	271	until	37	298
looking	41	272	drink	36	299
woods	41	273	ground	36	300
brought	40	274	holiday	36	301
coming	40	275	left	36	302
forest	40	276	open	36	303
live	40	277	seen	36	304
much	40	278	wheel	36	305
pool	40	279	won	36	306
sky	40	280	before	35	307
snow	40	281	caught	35	308
brown	39	282	every	35	309
can't	39	283	fly	35	310
cup	39	284	kept	35	311
happy	39	285	last	35	312
moon	39	286	toys	35	313
paper	39	287	which	35	314
sun	39	288	air	34	315
swimming	39	289	animals	34	316
bedroom	38	290	any	34	317
inside	38	291	doing	34	318
scared	38	292	game	34	319
snooker	38	293	I'll	34	320
years	38	294	nose	34	321
birthday	37	295	ok	34	322

please	34	323	new	31	350
stuck	34	324	picked	31	351
treasure	34	325	someone	31	352
felt	33	326	unhappy	31	353
five	33	327	bike	30	354
flowers	33	328	book	30	355
four	33	329	box	30	356
grass	33	330	grew	30	357
land	33	331	half	30	358
nearly	33	332	happened	30	359
police	33	333	happily	30	360
used	33	334	knew	30	361
yesterday	33	335	lunch	30	362
been	32	336	monster	30	363
done	32	337	myself	30	364
fast	32	338	place	30	365
front	32	339	turn	30	366
ghost	32	340	wolf	30	367
rabbit	32	341	along	29	368
sat	32	342	decided	29	369
shouted	32	343	fox	29	370
under	32	344	free	29	371
bag	31	345	hard	29	372
boys	31	346	golden	29	373
girls	31	347	past	29	374
golden	31	348	same	29	375
hand	31	349	shed	29	376

today	29	377	rat	27	404
town	29	378	shoes	27	405
couldn't	28	379	Sunday	27	406
dry	28	380	sweets	27	407
hospital	28	381	world	27	408
landed	28	382	beach	26	409
stay	28	383	better	26	410
together	28	384	breakfast	26	411
asleep	27	385	class	26	412
birds	27	386	eggs	26	413
bought	27	387	fun	26	414
cake	27	388	hat	26	415
changed	27	389	hill	26	416
climbed	27	390	killed	26	417
days	27	391	noise	26	418
dead	27	392	really	26	419
everyone	27	393	stop	26	420
great	27	394	that's	26	421
grow	27	395	wall	26	422
hot	27	396	while	26	423
knocked	27	397	cow	25	424
legs	27	398	hello	25	425
light	27	399	leaves	25	426
lovely	27	400	love	25	427
near	27	401	milk	25	428
princess	27	402	mouse	25	429
race	27	403	set	25	430

threw	25	431	horse	23	458
wish	25	432	keep	23	459
beans	24	433	makes	23	460
bear	24	434	nest	23	461
broke	24	435	pulled	23	462
downstairs	24	436	sand	23	463
family	24	437	snake	23	464
getting	24	438	ten	23	465
houses	24	439	than	23	466
o'clock	24	440	woman	23	467
piece	24	441	broomstick	23	468
pink	24	442	dance	22	469
ready	24	443	fairy	22	470
ship	24	444	funny	22	471
space	24	445	let's	22	472
stayed	24	446	lighthouse	22	473
ago	24	447	lion	22	474
alright	23	448	met	22	475
apple	23	449	miss	22	476
began	23	450	party	22	477
cut	23	451	says	22	478
died	23	452	secret	22	479
dinosaurs	23	453	show	22	480
each	23	454	Shrove-Tuesday	22	481
even	23	455	small	22	482
eye	23	456	stairs	22	483
favourite	23	457	teeth	22	484

13

trying	22	485		different	20	512
upstairs	22	486		dressed	20	513
watch	22	487		duck	20	514
week	22	488		everything	20	515
wool	22	489		fall	20	516
year	22	490		Friday	20	517
behind	22	491		haunted	20	518
bottle	21	492		himself	20	519
cars	21	493		horrible	20	520
full	21	494		jungle	20	521
hit	21	495		names	20	522
kind	21	496		path	20	523
making	21	497		presents	20	524
middle	21	498		ring	20	525
must	21	499		shops	20	526
own	21	500		table	20	527
rain	21	501		thank	20	528
river	21	502		there's	20	529
rocket	21	503		tunnel	20	530
talk	21	504		visit	20	531
tower	21	505		wait	20	532
train	21	506		ask	19	533
ate	20	507		catch	19	534
ball	20	508		cousin	19	535
bang	20	509		dear	19	536
bus	20	510		egg	19	537
buy	20	511		field	19	538

flower	19	539		orange	18	566
foot	19	540		pig	18	567
grandad	19	541		quickly	18	568
hands	19	542		say	18	569
ice-cream	19	543		showed	18	570
jump	19	544		stone	18	571
leg	19	545		swim	18	572
life	19	546		teacher	18	573
machine	19	547		toad	18	574
monkey	19	548		waited	17	575
newspaper	19	549		Ash-Wednesday	17	576
rainbow	19	550		being	17	577
running	19	551		bottom	17	578
seed	19	552		bring	17	579
summer	19	553		comes	17	580
talking	19	554		face	17	581
yellow	19	555		followed	17	582
baron	18	556		hold	17	583
coach	18	557		I've	17	584
cried	18	558		jar	17	585
does	18	559		ladies	17	586
doll	18	560		later	17	587
frightened	18	561		lights	17	588
laughed	18	562		mum's	17	589
most	18	563		nothing	17	590
mouth	18	564		pick	17	591
ones	18	565		pin	17	592

pushed	17	593	pub	16	620
quite	17	594	shopping	16	621
rest	17	595	spaceship	16	622
robot	17	596	spell	16	623
seeds	17	597	storm	16	624
straight	17	598	tiger	16	625
watched	17	599	vet	16	626
young	16	600	watching	15	627
balloons	16	601	Winter	15	628
blew	16	602	across	15	629
course	16	603	beard	15	630
crooked	16	604	beautiful	15	631
crying	16	605	blow	15	632
devil	16	606	clean	15	633
dream	16	607	coat	15	634
dropped	16	608	crashed	15	635
everybody	16	609	daughter	15	636
feet	16	610	dress	15	637
fight	16	611	feathers	15	638
floor	16	612	flying	15	639
having	16	613	guess	15	640
high	16	614	honey	15	641
key	16	615	kitchen	15	642
magician	16	616	lead	15	643
planet	16	617	locked	15	644
plays	16	618	loved	15	645
pounds	16	619	many	15	646

means	15	647	climb	14	674
mole	15	648	colours	14	675
moved	15	649	cotton	14	676
pet	15	650	cousins	14	677
present	15	651	covered	14	678
sent	15	652	crept	14	679
shut	15	653	dad's	14	680
slept	15	654	doors	14	681
stick	15	655	faster	14	682
street	15	656	feather	14	683
stuff	15	657	fruit	14	684
till	15	658	hid	14	685
times	15	659	idea	14	686
vegetables	15	660	instead	14	687
wear	15	661	island	14	688
wears	15	662	knight	14	689
whole	15	663	late	14	690
wife	14	664	laughing	14	691
wrong	14	665	lives	14	692
also	14	666	maid	14	693
anything	14	667	painted	14	694
arm	14	668	picnic	14	695
babies	14	669	playground	14	696
badger	14	670	pot	14	697
both	14	671	rocks	14	698
call	14	672	sack	14	699
change	14	673	safe	14	700

second	14	701		frog	13	728
should	14	702		games	13	729
silver	14	703		gets	13	730
slowly	14	704		goals	13	731
somebody	14	705		granny	13	732
those	14	706		hear	13	733
tired	14	707		helped	13	734
tomorrow	14	708		hunt	13	735
uncle	14	709		ice	13	736
wash	14	710		lake	13	737
wasn't	14	711		Lego	13	738
wearing	14	712		letter	13	739
windows	13	713		lorry	13	740
wings	13	714		mad	13	741
bigger	13	715		Monday	13	742
born	13	716		oranges	13	743
break	13	717		pen	13	744
built	13	718		policemen	13	745
chips	13	719		rescue	13	746
dancing	13	720		ride	13	747
deep	13	721		scarf	13	748
die	13	722		seaside	13	749
dogs	13	723		seven	13	750
drank	13	724		shall	13	751
earth	13	725		sisters	13	752
fat	13	726		size	13	753
few	13	727		team	13	754

Thursday	13	755	might	12	782
trap	13	756	minutes	12	783
try	13	757	packed	12	784
use	12	758	pancake	12	785
aeroplane	12	759	plane	12	786
appeared	12	760	pond	12	787
bees	12	761	ponies	12	788
blind	12	762	postman	12	789
bridge	12	763	queen	12	790
butter	12	764	read	12	791
carried	12	765	rock	12	792
clouds	12	766	scored	12	793
colour	12	767	short	12	794
disco	12	768	shot	12	795
drove	12	769	sing	12	796
except	12	770	sit	12	797
falling	12	771	skin	12	798
far	12	772	smack	12	799
farm	12	773	sorry	12	800
feel	12	774	sound	12	801
grey	12	775	swings	12	802
gun	12	776	tail	12	803
hour	12	777	takes	12	804
hurt	12	778	teddy	12	805
likes	12	779	these	12	806
married	12	780	village	12	807
may	12	781	walls	12	808

warm	12	809		knock	11	836
what's	12	810		learn	11	837
wild	12	811		led	11	838
win	12	812		looks	11	839
adventure	11	813		metal	11	840
alive	11	814		nan's	11	841
animal	11	815		others	11	842
ashes	11	816		pancakes	11	843
assembly	11	817		pencil	11	844
became	11	818		person	11	845
blood	11	819		policeman	11	846
bread	11	820		poor	11	847
bright	11	821		post	11	848
burst	11	822		rolled	11	849
caravan	11	823		rope	11	850
caterpillar	11	824		sang	11	851
cats	11	825		score	11	852
cream	11	826		singing	11	853
cry	11	827		song	11	854
engine	11	828		soup	11	855
fed	11	829		special	11	856
flood	11	830		stones	11	857
grandma	11	831		stood	11	858
heads	11	832		strange	11	859
ill	11	833		tall	11	860
king's	11	834		television	11	861
kite	11	835		theatre	11	862

twenty	11	863	match	10	890
worms	11	864	meat	10	891
angry	10	865	mind	10	892
ark	10	866	nan	10	893
army	10	867	need	10	894
bell	10	868	nine	10	895
branch	10	869	onto	10	896
build	10	870	picture	10	897
carrots	10	871	pretty	10	898
classroom	10	872	rabbits	10	899
competition	10	873	sell	10	900
computer	10	874	shoot	10	901
decorations	10	875	sins	10	902
dug	10	876	squirrel	10	903
eight	10	877	station	10	904
gate	10	878	stole	10	905
glad	10	879	sunny	10	906
goal	10	880	torch	10	907
hall	10	881	towel	10	908
headmaster	10	882	toy	10	909
helicopter	10	883	trip	10	910
hours	10	884	waiting	10	911
hut	10	885	wake	10	912
job	10	886	wet	9	913
letters	10	887	wished	9	914
living	10	888	acrobat	9	915
map	10	889	age	9	916

apples	9	917	giant's	9	944
bits	9	918	growing	9	945
bluetit	9	919	he's	9	946
bull	9	920	held	9	947
burglar	9	921	hungry	9	948
buttons	9	922	jumper	9	949
candyfloss	9	923	keeper	9	950
cannot	9	924	kicked	9	951
case	9	925	ladder	9	952
chocolate	9	926	line	9	953
church	9	927	lions	9	954
circus	9	928	lucky	9	955
cottage	9	929	man's	9	956
disappeared	9	930	mine	9	957
drive	9	931	moment	9	958
dust	9	932	named	9	959
ears	9	933	office	9	960
eats	9	934	peas	9	961
elephant	9	935	pieces	9	962
elf	9	936	pirates	9	963
else	9	937	pleased	9	964
escaped	9	938	potion	9	965
feed	9	939	quick	9	966
feeling	9	940	quiet	9	967
fishing	9	941	reach	9	968
friendly	9	942	robin	9	969
garage	9	943	roof	9	970

saved	9	971	bats	8	998
shark	9	972	believe	8	999
silly	9	973	biscuits	8	1000
sitting	9	974	bow	8	1001
six	9	975	button	8	1002
smoke	9	976	cage	8	1003
sort	9	977	cards	8	1004
strong	9	978	carpet	8	1005
swam	9	979	chest	8	1006
tonight	9	980	close	8	1007
tricks	9	981	cloud	8	1008
trousers	9	982	cook	8	1009
true	9	983	cornflakes	8	1010
van	9	984	country	8	1011
wedding	9	985	cross	8	1012
Wednesday	9	986	dirty	8	1013
wicked	9	987	diver	8	1014
wizard	9	988	doesn't	8	1015
wondered	9	989	dreamed	8	1016
woolly	9	990	early	8	1017
works	9	991	easy	8	1018
address	8	992	everywhere	8	1019
against	8	993	ferry	8	1020
anyone	8	994	fierce	8	1021
attacked	8	995	fine	8	1022
auntie	8	996	fired	8	1023
ballet	8	997	forgot	8	1024

ghosts	8	1025	puppies	8	1052
gives	8	1026	putting	8	1053
goldfish	8	1027	rained	8	1054
goose	8	1028	rang	8	1055
grandmother	8	1029	remember	8	1056
grown	8	1030	riding	8	1057
heavy	8	1031	row	8	1058
higher	8	1032	rowing	8	1059
hills	8	1033	runs	8	1060
holidays	8	1034	sailor	8	1061
hoop	8	1035	shouting	8	1062
hope	8	1036	shrinking	8	1063
hundred	8	1037	sign	8	1064
jumping	8	1038	slide	8	1065
lay	8	1039	socks	8	1066
leave	8	1040	spider	8	1067
meet	8	1041	spinning	8	1068
melted	8	1042	stand	8	1069
mud	8	1043	start	8	1070
neck	8	1044	though	8	1071
normal	8	1045	towards	8	1072
number	8	1046	TV	8	1073
paint	8	1047	v (= versus)	8	1074
parents	8	1048	washed	8	1075
planted	8	1049	washing	8	1076
politicians	8	1050	weasels	8	1077
prince	8	1051	witches	8	1078

won't	8	1079	destroyed	7	1106
wonder	8	1080	donkey	7	1107
wouldn't	8	1081	drinks	7	1108
write	8	1082	eaten	7	1109
afternoon	7	1083	eating	7	1110
already	7	1084	elephants	7	1111
arms	7	1085	empty	7	1112
aunt	7	1086	fighting	7	1113
bedtime	7	1087	film	7	1114
boastful	7	1088	final	7	1115
books	7	1089	flat	7	1116
bored	7	1090	following	7	1117
bumper-cars	7	1091	glass	7	1118
busy	7	1092	glasses	7	1119
cakes	7	1093	goat	7	1120
careful	7	1094	gran	7	1121
chair	7	1095	granny's	7	1122
chairs	7	1096	hotel	7	1123
chase	7	1097	hunting	7	1124
child	7	1098	kick	7	1125
circle	7	1099	kingdom	7	1126
clown	7	1100	lit	7	1127
coffee	7	1101	lonely	7	1128
coloured	7	1102	marry	7	1129
corner	7	1103	mathematician	7	1130
crown	7	1104	matter	7	1131
cubs	7	1105	mean	7	1132

miles	7	1133	spooky	7	1160
model	7	1134	squeak	7	1161
monsters	7	1135	standing	7	1162
motorbike	7	1136	stickers	7	1163
mountains	7	1137	sticks	7	1164
music	7	1138	sugar	7	1165
olden	7	1139	supper	7	1166
owl	7	1140	sweet	7	1167
owner	7	1141	swing	7	1168
panic	7	1142	tent	7	1169
pop	7	1143	tigers	7	1170
pound	7	1144	touched	7	1171
pressed	7	1145	trains	7	1172
prison	7	1146	trouble	7	1173
pull	7	1147	tube	7	1174
remembered	7	1148	twigs	7	1175
robbers	7	1149	umbrella	7	1176
rockets	7	1150	wallpaper	7	1177
seal	7	1151	wide	7	1178
send	7	1152	windy	7	1179
sewer	7	1153	wore	7	1180
sharp	7	1154	worked	7	1181
shone	7	1155	you're	7	1182
smash	7	1156	aeroplanes	7	1183
soft	7	1157	afraid	6	1184
spade	7	1158	ambulance	6	1185
spirit	7	1159	angel	6	1186

anyway	6	1187	crisps	6	1214
arches	6	1188	daddy's	6	1215
aren't	6	1189	deer	6	1216
arrow	6	1190	doctor	6	1217
badgers	6	1191	dreaming	6	1218
bananas	6	1192	driver	6	1219
beside	6	1193	enjoy	6	1220
bite	6	1194	enough	6	1221
blanket	6	1195	excited	6	1222
bobble	6	1196	exciting	6	1223
boots	6	1197	fairies	6	1224
brick	6	1198	fence	6	1225
brother's	6	1199	filled	6	1226
building	6	1200	finger	6	1227
bump	6	1201	fog	6	1228
bumped	6	1202	forever	6	1229
bush	6	1203	forward	6	1230
butterfly	6	1204	gardens	6	1231
calling	6	1205	goodbye	6	1232
ceiling	6	1206	grabbed	6	1233
cell	6	1207	hairdresser	6	1234
cheese	6	1208	hanging	6	1235
chick	6	1209	haven't	6	1236
chopped	6	1210	hay	6	1237
commando	6	1211	hung	6	1238
control	6	1212	isn't	6	1239
crash	6	1213	jelly	6	1240

jet	6	1241	questions	6	1268
June	6	1242	reading	6	1269
kings	6	1243	real	6	1270
least	6	1244	rich	6	1271
lesson	6	1245	roads	6	1272
lines	6	1246	roots	6	1273
mail	6	1247	rose	6	1274
maybe	6	1248	rough	6	1275
meant	6	1249	saying	6	1276
meanwhile	6	1250	scary	6	1277
mice	6	1251	shaking	6	1278
museum	6	1252	sheep	6	1279
nail	6	1253	sick	6	1280
nanna	6	1254	silence	6	1281
nanny	6	1255	skirt	6	1282
nasty	6	1256	slipped	6	1283
naughty	6	1257	smell	6	1284
nobody	6	1258	smooth	6	1285
none	6	1259	snakes	6	1286
palace	6	1260	soggy	6	1287
phoned	6	1261	soldier	6	1288
picking	6	1262	sorts	6	1289
plant	6	1263	spiders	6	1290
potato	6	1264	split	6	1291
press	6	1265	spots	6	1292
pulling	6	1266	star	6	1293
quarter	6	1267	suppose	6	1294

sure	6	1295	answer	5	1322
surprise	6	1296	ash	5	1323
sword	6	1297	axe	5	1324
tables	6	1298	bags	5	1325
teachers	6	1299	balls	5	1326
they're	6	1300	bar	5	1327
tied	6	1301	bars	5	1328
tissue	6	1302	bath	5	1329
tortoise	6	1303	beast	5	1330
tunnels	6	1304	beat	5	1331
twisted	6	1305	bee	5	1332
unlocked	6	1306	bells	5	1333
vanished	6	1307	biggest	5	1334
voice	6	1308	body	5	1335
washing-up	6	1309	bonfire	5	1336
weren't	6	1310	bowl	5	1337
whisper	6	1311	boy's	5	1338
witch's	6	1312	breath	5	1339
without	6	1313	broken	5	1340
word	6	1314	buzzing	5	1341
working	6	1315	captain	5	1342
worried	6	1316	centre	5	1343
above	5	1317	chalk	5	1344
accident	5	1318	champion	5	1345
act	5	1319	chased	5	1346
advisers	5	1320	chicken	5	1347
alone	5	1321	Christmas-Eve	5	1348

climbing	5	1349	hardly	5	1376
clock	5	1350	hare	5	1377
club	5	1351	herself	5	1378
coats	5	1352	hide	5	1379
cooking	5	1353	hiding	5	1380
couple	5	1354	hitting	5	1381
cub	5	1355	holding	5	1382
cupboard	5	1356	holes	5	1383
deal	5	1357	I'd	5	1384
dinosaur	5	1358	indeed	5	1385
dragged	5	1359	insects	5	1386
draw	5	1360	invent	5	1387
drew	5	1361	invention	5	1388
drunk	5	1362	invited	5	1389
Easter	5	1363	jolly	5	1390
ended	5	1364	journey	5	1391
evil	5	1365	juicy	5	1392
eyebrows	5	1366	kettle	5	1393
fairground	5	1367	kill	5	1394
fallen	5	1368	kiss	5	1395
fingers	5	1369	kittens	5	1396
follow	5	1370	lane	5	1397
friend's	5	1371	logs	5	1398
gardener	5	1372	lorries	5	1399
guessed	5	1373	loud	5	1400
gymnast	5	1374	lower	5	1401
happen	5	1375	lying	5	1402

March	5	1403		pirate	5	1430
marks	5	1404		plan	5	1431
master	5	1405		plants	5	1432
mat	5	1406		player	5	1433
meeting	5	1407		pocket	5	1434
miaow	5	1408		poem	5	1435
metres	5	1409		polish	5	1436
minute	5	1410		popped	5	1437
missed	5	1411		poster	5	1438
mixed	5	1412		potatoes	5	1439
months	5	1413		powder	5	1440
mother's	5	1414		pudding	5	1441
move	5	1415		puff	5	1442
moving	5	1416		rains	5	1443
mummy's	5	1417		roses	5	1444
needed	5	1418		rushed	5	1445
normally	5	1419		sale	5	1446
notice	5	1420		sandwiches	5	1447
nuts	5	1421		scream	5	1448
oil	5	1422		shape	5	1449
oldest	5	1423		sheet	5	1450
paid	5	1424		shells	5	1451
pass	5	1425		sheriff	5	1452
passed	5	1426		shirt	5	1453
pedal	5	1427		shook	5	1454
phone	5	1428		shooting	5	1455
pictures	5	1429		shore	5	1456

sight	5	1457	waiter	5	1484
sleeping	5	1458	war	5	1485
smashed	5	1459	waved	5	1486
smiled	5	1460	waves	5	1487
somewhere	5	1461	weapons	5	1488
songs	5	1462	weeks	5	1489
spokes	5	1463	werewolf	5	1490
squashed	5	1464	whiskey	5	1491
stepped	5	1465	wondering	5	1492
stream	5	1466	yet	5	1493
streets	5	1467	you've	5	1494
string	5	1468	able	4	1495
switch	5	1469	ah	4	1496
switched	5	1470	ahead	4	1497
taking	5	1471	airport	4	1498
teams	5	1472	alarm	4	1499
tells	5	1473	alien	4	1500
terrible	5	1474	allowed	4	1501
thinking	5	1475	almost	4	1502
thunder	5	1476	amazing	4	1503
tip	5	1477	anymore	4	1504
tooth	5	1478	arch	4	1505
trapped	5	1479	arrived	4	1506
trick	5	1480	awake	4	1507
tripped	5	1481	bank	4	1508
Tuesday	5	1482	bathroom	4	1509
voices	5	1483	battle	4	1510

beak	4	1511	changes	4	1538
bears	4	1512	changing	4	1539
beginning	4	1513	charge	4	1540
between	4	1514	chasing	4	1541
biscuit	4	1515	checked	4	1542
blizzard	4	1516	cherry	4	1543
board	4	1517	city	4	1544
bolognese	4	1518	clay	4	1545
bomb	4	1519	closed	4	1546
boot	4	1520	closer	4	1547
border	4	1521	cloth	4	1548
braille	4	1522	clowns	4	1549
branches	4	1523	coins	4	1550
brave	4	1524	collar	4	1551
breathe	4	1525	collected	4	1552
broomsticks	4	1526	cool	4	1553
brothers	4	1527	countries	4	1554
brush	4	1528	cover	4	1555
buns	4	1529	cows	4	1556
burnt	4	1530	crazy	4	1557
bushes	4	1531	curved	4	1558
cable-car	4	1532	darts	4	1559
captured	4	1533	deeper	4	1560
care	4	1534	describing	4	1561
carrot	4	1535	desert	4	1562
caterpillars	4	1536	difficult	4	1563
chains	4	1537	dip	4	1564

dog's	4	1565	finishing	4	1592
dolly	4	1566	fir	4	1593
dot	4	1567	fit	4	1594
double	4	1568	flamingo	4	1595
double-decker	4	1569	flashing	4	1596
dried	4	1570	float	4	1597
driving	4	1571	floated	4	1598
drowned	4	1572	flour	4	1599
ducks	4	1573	flown	4	1600
dusty	4	1574	forgiven	4	1601
eagle	4	1575	forgotten	4	1602
either	4	1576	forms	4	1603
enchanter	4	1577	freckles	4	1604
enjoyed	4	1578	Fridays	4	1605
enormous	4	1579	frizzed	4	1606
everyday	4	1580	further	4	1607
exercise	4	1581	gap	4	1608
exploded	4	1582	gates	4	1609
factory	4	1583	ghoul	4	1610
fainted	4	1584	gingerbread	4	1611
fake	4	1585	girl's	4	1612
fantastic	4	1586	gobbled	4	1613
farmer	4	1587	grandfather	4	1614
fibreglass	4	1588	group	4	1615
fields	4	1589	guide	4	1616
fights	4	1590	hanky-panky	4	1617
finally	4	1591	harp	4	1618

hate	4	1619		lets	4	1646
hats	4	1620		lid	4	1647
hen	4	1621		lift	4	1648
horses	4	1622		lifted	4	1649
huge	4	1623		lighthouses	4	1650
hunted	4	1624		longship	4	1651
hurry	4	1625		low	4	1652
imp	4	1626		luckily	4	1653
inn	4	1627		mate	4	1654
interesting	4	1628		midnight	4	1655
iron	4	1629		millions	4	1656
jacket	4	1630		misty	4	1657
jobs	4	1631		mittens	4	1658
juice	4	1632		mix	4	1659
killer	4	1633		monkeys	4	1660
kissed	4	1634		moonlight	4	1661
kitten	4	1635		mothers	4	1662
knee	4	1636		mountain	4	1663
ladybirds	4	1637		nearer	4	1664
lambs	4	1638		news	4	1665
large	4	1639		nil	4	1666
laugh	4	1640		noises	4	1667
lazy	4	1641		noticed	4	1668
leader	4	1642		nowhere	4	1669
learned	4	1643		ocean	4	1670
lemonade	4	1644		octopus	4	1671
Lent	4	1645		paddle	4	1672

pair	4	1673	reward	4	1700
papier-mache	4	1674	rings	4	1701
part	4	1675	roared	4	1702
paste	4	1676	rode	4	1703
paws	4	1677	roll	4	1704
petrol	4	1678	ropes	4	1705
pets	4	1679	rusty	4	1706
pipe	4	1680	sailed	4	1707
places	4	1681	sandwich	4	1708
pony	4	1682	screamed	4	1709
postcode	4	1683	seats	4	1710
pots	4	1684	selfish	4	1711
poured	4	1685	sells	4	1712
prey	4	1686	servants	4	1713
priest	4	1687	share	4	1714
primroses	4	1688	shoe	4	1715
probably	4	1689	shoulder	4	1716
programme	4	1690	sides	4	1717
punk	4	1691	sister's	4	1718
puppy	4	1692	sixty	4	1719
queen's	4	1693	skating	4	1720
racing	4	1694	slaves	4	1721
raining	4	1695	sledging	4	1722
rather	4	1696	slip	4	1723
reached	4	1697	slugs	4	1724
realized	4	1698	smile	4	1725
rescued	4	1699	snapped	4	1726

snowing	4	1727		talked	4	1754
snowman's	4	1728		tasted	4	1755
son	4	1729		temple	4	1756
spaghetti	4	1730		test	4	1757
spells	4	1731		themselves	4	1758
spoke	4	1732		thin	4	1759
spoon	4	1733		throw	4	1760
spray	4	1734		thrown	4	1761
spring	4	1735		tidy	4	1762
spy	4	1736		toast	4	1763
starting	4	1737		tomato	4	1764
staying	4	1738		turns	4	1765
stays	4	1739		twelve	4	1766
steal	4	1740		twig	4	1767
steps	4	1741		underground	4	1768
sticky	4	1742		viper	4	1769
straw	4	1743		visited	4	1770
strawberries	4	1744		wand	4	1771
stupid	4	1745		we're	4	1772
style	4	1746		we've	4	1773
such	4	1747		weekend	4	1774
sudden	4	1748		whale	4	1775
super	4	1749		wheels	4	1776
surface	4	1750		whoever	4	1777
swan	4	1751		wine	4	1778
tadpoles	4	1752		wolves	4	1779
taken	4	1753		wonderful	4	1780

words	4	1781	brock	3	1808
adults	3	1782	brontosaurus	3	1809
adventures	3	1783	broom	3	1810
aimed	3	1784	bubbles	3	1811
allosaurus	3	1785	budgie	3	1812
ant	3	1786	bull's	3	1813
apartment	3	1787	bulldog	3	1814
arrows	3	1788	bunk-bed	3	1815
aunty	3	1789	bunk-beds	3	1816
awful	3	1790	bye	3	1817
badge	3	1791	cabbage	3	1818
baked	3	1792	calls	3	1819
barber	3	1793	calm	3	1820
bark	3	1794	candy	3	1821
basket	3	1795	cardboard	3	1822
bat	3	1796	Care-bear	3	1823
batteries	3	1797	Care-bears	3	1824
beds	3	1798	cart	3	1825
belonged	3	1799	catching	3	1826
below	3	1800	caused	3	1827
berries	3	1801	cavemen	3	1828
bin	3	1802	caves	3	1829
blast	3	1803	chance	3	1830
blowing	3	1804	children's	3	1831
bombs	3	1805	chocolates	3	1832
bones	3	1806	classrooms	3	1833
boom	3	1807	cleaned	3	1834

cleaning	3	1835	diamond	3	1862
clear	3	1836	dies	3	1863
clicked	3	1837	diplodocus	3	1864
Coke	3	1838	dipped	3	1865
condor	3	1839	disaster	3	1866
cooks	3	1840	dishes	3	1867
corn	3	1841	diving	3	1868
cot	3	1842	dizzy	3	1869
counted	3	1843	dresses	3	1870
cracked	3	1844	dressing	3	1871
creatures	3	1845	dungeon	3	1872
creep	3	1846	during	3	1873
crew	3	1847	easily	3	1874
crocodile	3	1848	eaters	3	1875
crossing	3	1849	edge	3	1876
crowd	3	1850	eleven	3	1877
cruel	3	1851	especially	3	1878
curry	3	1852	evaporates	3	1879
curtain	3	1853	eventually	3	1880
dangerous	3	1854	explore	3	1881
darker	3	1855	fabric	3	1882
daylight	3	1856	faces	3	1883
death	3	1857	fact	3	1884
delighted	3	1858	famous	3	1885
deliver	3	1859	Father-Christmas	3	1886
delivered	3	1860	feast	3	1887
destroy	3	1861	feeding	3	1888

female	3	1889	heart	3	1917
fireworks	3	1890	helter-skelter	3	1918
flats	3	1891	here's	3	1919
floors	3	1892	homes	3	1920
footprints	3	1893	homework	3	1921
fright	3	1894	horror	3	1922
frightening	3	1895	horsemeat	3	1923
frogs	3	1896	hose	3	1924
furry	3	1897	humans	3	1925
future	3	1898	hunter	3	1926
garbage	3	1899	hutch	3	1927
gardening	3	1900	important	3	1928
gas	3	1901	invader	3	1929
giggling	3	1902	invisible	3	1930
glared	3	1903	ivy	3	1031
glue	3	1904	jail	3	1932
godmother	3	1905	jig	3	1933
grannie	3	1906	join	3	1934
great-tit	3	1907	joined	3	1935
grocers	3	1908	joy	3	1936
guard	3	1909	July	3	1937
gulls	3	1910	jumpers	3	1938
hadn't	3	1911	kicking	3	1939
halfway	3	1912	kinds	3	1940
hammerhead	3	1913	kit	3	1941
handle	3	1914	knife	3	1942
hang	3	1915	knights	3	1943
heap	3	1916	lamb	3	1944

landing	3	1945	needle	3	1973
laser	3	1946	needs	3	1974
lawn	3	1947	neither	3	1975
learning	3	1948	nests	3	1976
leopards	3	1949	netball	3	1977
lifeboat	3	1950	nibble	3	1978
lifts	3	1951	nights	3	1979
lama	3	1952	November	3	1980
local	3	1953	numbers	3	1981
log	3	1954	nut	3	1982
longer	3	1955	oars	3	1983
lose	3	1956	obstacle	3	1984
magicked	3	1957	operation	3	1985
mallard	3	1958	ordinary	3	1986
mammoth	3	1959	outing	3	1987
mammy	3	1960	oven	3	1988
managed	3	1961	overboard	3	1989
manager	3	1962	owned	3	1990
mare	3	1963	paddled	3	1991
margarine	3	1964	paddling	3	1992
market	3	1965	paw	3	1993
mayor	3	1966	penalty	3	1994
mechanic	3	1967	pensioners	3	1995
mile	3	1968	people's	3	1996
mill	3	1969	plain	3	1997
mystery	3	1970	planned	3	1998
nearest	3	1971	plastic	3	1999
neat	3	1972	Plasticine	3	2000

The Top 2,000 Words Used By 8-Year Olds In Their Writing

Word	Frequency	Rank	Word	Frequency	Rank
the	11620	1	up	1181	27
and	11084	2	but	1121	28
I	7025	3	me	1101	29
a	6610	4	with	1057	30
to	5708	5	go	1048	31
was	4204	6	for	1044	32
it	3602	7	that	1041	33
we	3312	8	out	992	34
in	3115	9	at	960	35
my	2684	10	have	952	36
he	2633	11	day	929	37
went	2516	12	some	863	38
of	2340	13	all	823	39
then	2097	14	were	810	40
on	2067	15	his	796	41
said	2050	16	her	763	42
they	1903	17	like	763	43
had	1686	18	are	743	44
is	1673	19	came	728	45
she	1602	20	saw	720	46
got	1428	21	mum	718	47
when	1423	22	home	680	48
there	1365	23	back	674	49
you	1337	24	get	636	50
so	1302	25	not	601	51
one	1283	26	down	599	52

very	597	53	off	369	80
into	568	54	school	354	81
because	555	55	after	352	82
them	555	56	took	347	83
him	519	57	if	345	84
would	506	58	from	344	85
be	493	59	man	342	86
put	492	60	has	338	87
called	472	61	an	335	88
time	468	62	us	331	89
our	457	63	about	330	90
what	454	64	ran	316	91
house	452	65	next	315	92
as	447	66	found	313	93
will	437	67	their	313	94
little	422	68	bed	303	95
can	415	69	am	302	96
big	408	70	play	298	97
could	395	71	door	296	98
see	388	72	over	295	99
going	386	73	good	285	100
people	385	74	your	285	101
dad	379	75	this	281	102
two	379	76	made	280	103
come	375	77	by	267	104
did	374	78	yes	260	105
do	371	79	no	257	106

just	252	107	through	190	134
other	246	108	don't	188	135
night	245	109	car	185	136
again	241	110	make	185	137
looked	240	111	friend	182	138
water	238	112	three	182	139
old	235	113	tree	182	140
lots	233	114	ghost	180	141
told	232	115	lived	180	142
way	228	116	didn't	178	143
who	228	117	how	174	144
started	225	118	thought	174	145
away	223	119	food	173	146
first	222	120	long	172	147
morning	217	121	dog	171	148
name	216	122	things	170	149
well	216	123	know	169	150
now	215	124	played	169	151
where	215	125	girl	166	152
room	210	126	take	166	153
heard	209	127	want	166	154
once	209	128	boy	161	155
look	206	129	Mrs	161	156
too	198	130	nice	161	157
friends	196	131	or	158	158
fell	192	132	wood	158	159
round	191	133	tea	156	160

find	155	161		eat	128	188
fire	152	162		white	128	189
suddenly	152	163		left	126	190
coming	148	164		opened	126	191
children	147	165		sea	126	192
another	146	166		walking	126	193
gave	145	167		blue	125	194
woke	144	168		walked	125	195
been	143	169		window	125	196
dinner	143	170		asked	122	197
brother	142	171		Christmas	122	198
cat	142	172		live	122	199
best	141	173		shop	120	200
sister	138	174		end	119	201
which	135	175		bit	118	202
sometimes	134	176		oh	118	203
garden	133	177		set	118	204
gold	131	178		before	117	205
here	131	179		never	117	206
lot	131	180		only	117	207
something	131	181		soon	117	208
around	130	182		help	116	209
black	130	183		right	116	210
playing	130	184		sleep	116	211
walk	130	185		dragon	113	212
happy	129	186		magic	113	213
more	129	187		top	113	214

work	113	215	lost	99	242
getting	112	216	money	99	243
much	112	217	wish	99	244
red	111	218	trees	98	245
I'm	110	219	witch	98	246
think	109	220	eyes	97	247
mummy	108	221	football	97	248
class	107	222	green	97	249
it's	107	223	park	97	250
fish	106	224	why	96	251
outside	106	225	new	95	252
upon	106	226	always	94	253
gone	105	227	every	94	254
last	105	228	family	94	255
baby	104	229	inside	94	256
hole	104	230	ball	93	257
dark	103	231	birthday	92	258
jumped	103	232	let	92	259
thing	103	233	cold	91	260
wanted	103	234	its	90	261
cave	102	235	tried	90	262
past	102	236	half	89	263
still	102	237	stopped	89	264
under	102	238	any	88	265
Mr	101	239	goes	88	266
looking	100	240	turned	88	267
head	99	241	behind	87	268

box	87	269	swimming	76	296
lady	87	270	used	75	297
fun	86	271	world	74	298
let's	85	272	air	73	299
caught	84	273	bedroom	73	300
mother	84	274	bird	73	301
years	84	275	died	73	302
different	82	276	five	73	303
hair	82	277	four	73	304
rabbit	82	278	giant	73	305
turn	82	279	liked	73	306
drink	81	280	police	73	307
each	81	281	ready	73	308
really	81	282	side	73	309
lunch	79	283	won	73	310
please	79	284	scared	72	311
book	78	285	stop	72	312
ever	78	286	together	72	313
road	78	287	face	71	314
days	77	288	forest	71	315
funny	77	289	hot	71	316
land	77	290	knew	71	317
open	77	291	sat	71	318
small	77	292	table	71	319
men	76	293	yellow	71	320
noise	76	294	hello	69	321
run	76	295	nearly	69	322

o'clock	69	323	father	65	350
say	69	324	light	65	351
ship	69	325	shot	65	352
birds	68	326	train	65	353
brown	68	327	asleep	64	354
doing	68	328	decided	64	355
lovely	68	329	front	64	356
tell	68	330	give	64	357
until	68	331	hit	64	358
couldn't	67	332	picked	64	359
finished	67	333	piece	64	360
happened	67	334	place	64	361
met	67	335	space	64	362
person	67	336	fly	63	363
downstairs	66	337	landed	63	364
egg	66	338	middle	63	365
felt	66	339	Saturday	63	366
flew	66	340	snow	63	367
grass	66	341	week	63	368
hard	66	342	while	63	369
sky	66	343	wind	63	370
sweets	66	344	along	62	371
that's	66	345	castle	62	372
upstairs	66	346	cut	62	373
woods	66	347	fast	62	374
breakfast	65	348	game	62	375
brought	65	349	great	62	376

rain	62	377	wasn't	58	404
teacher	62	378	bag	57	405
zoo	62	379	being	57	406
alright	61	380	few	57	407
boat	61	381	seal	57	408
kept	61	382	also	56	409
must	61	383	beach	56	410
someone	61	384	dressed	56	411
wheel	61	385	everything	56	412
animals	60	386	hospital	56	413
ate	60	387	party	56	414
bought	60	388	pond	56	415
ground	60	389	can't	55	416
seen	60	390	cup	55	417
stay	60	391	flowers	55	418
straight	60	392	hour	55	419
daddy	59	393	near	55	420
done	59	394	shouted	55	421
kind	59	395	story	55	422
myself	59	396	town	55	423
same	59	397	watch	55	424
Sunday	59	398	favourite	54	425
everybody	58	399	field	54	426
horse	58	400	games	54	427
most	58	401	holiday	54	428
paper	58	402	bus	53	429
six	58	403	comes	53	430

having	53	431	dead	49	458
king	53	432	keep	49	459
legs	53	433	should	49	460
music	53	434	eggs	48	461
own	53	435	flying	48	462
river	53	436	love	48	463
ten	53	437	O.K.	48	464
I've	53	438	quickly	48	465
bottom	52	439	ride	48	466
boys	52	440	showed	48	467
everyone	52	441	strange	48	468
floor	52	442	bear	47	469
full	52	443	nothing	47	470
miss	52	444	plane	47	471
pink	52	445	scored	47	472
better	51	446	stick	47	473
clothes	51	447	threw	47	474
even	51	448	warm	47	475
grandad	51	449	what's	47	476
running	51	450	I'll	47	477
secret	51	451	bike	46	478
fox	50	452	buy	46	479
later	50	453	girls	46	480
making	50	454	he's	46	481
second	50	455	lights	46	482
today	50	456	stayed	46	483
try	50	457	watched	46	484

call	45	485	anything	41	512
fat	45	486	city	41	513
happily	45	487	fairy	41	514
many	45	488	hear	41	515
mum's	45	489	ice	41	516
show	45	490	leg	41	517
teeth	45	491	mouse	41	518
pulled	44	492	names	41	519
tent	44	493	passed	41	520
than	44	494	quite	41	521
visit	44	495	start	41	522
voice	44	496	cake	40	523
catch	43	497	cars	40	524
hand	43	498	island	40	525
kill	43	499	sad	40	526
across	42	500	sit	40	527
country	42	501	stuck	40	528
might	42	502	winter	40	529
minutes	42	503	button	39	530
pick	42	504	does	39	531
pounds	42	505	dream	39	532
rest	42	506	Friday	39	533
shoes	42	507	killed	39	534
stairs	42	508	kitchen	39	535
summer	42	509	leaves	39	536
thank	42	510	moon	39	537
wait	42	511	path	39	538

presents	39	539		bang	36	566
sitting	39	540		climbed	36	567
year	39	541		colours	36	568
adventure	38	542		course	36	569
ago	38	543		crying	36	570
cupboard	38	544		dad's	36	571
dear	38	545		everywhere	36	572
fireworks	38	546		feet	36	573
grow	38	547		frightened	36	574
looks	38	548		grey	36	575
meat	38	549		hurt	36	576
minute	38	550		life	36	577
rock	38	551		lion	36	578
tail	38	552		machine	36	579
talking	38	553		monster	36	580
use	38	554		trip	35	581
wings	38	555		bad	35	582
blind	37	556		books	35	583
bottle	37	557		both	35	584
far	37	558		lives	35	585
key	37	559		need	35	586
letter	37	560		orange	35	587
milk	37	561		pet	35	588
pool	37	562		race	35	589
saying	37	563		read	35	590
sun	37	564		shall	35	591
you're	36	565		special	35	592

squirrel	35	593		clock	32	620
there's	34	594		dogs	32	621
arm	34	595		fall	32	622
dress	34	596		frog	32	623
feel	34	597		giants	32	624
followed	34	598		hall	32	625
idea	34	599		hold	32	626
makes	34	600		hope	32	627
monkey	34	601		hours	32	628
stone	33	602		instead	32	629
apple	33	603		knocked	32	630
blew	33	604		silly	32	631
broke	33	605		TV	32	632
built	33	606		witches	32	633
centre	33	607		believe	31	634
corner	33	608		bigger	31	635
himself	33	609		blood	31	636
playground	33	610		dancing	31	637
these	33	611		deep	31	638
till	33	612		dropped	31	639
wrong	33	613		ears	31	640
yesterday	32	614		foot	31	641
afternoon	32	615		leave	31	642
began	32	616		locked	31	643
bring	32	617		means	31	644
changed	32	618		move	31	645
classroom	32	619		pony	31	646

screamed	31	647	Monday	29	674
swim	31	648	sand	29	675
towards	31	649	sorry	29	676
waited	31	650	spaceship	29	677
wall	31	651	street	29	678
whole	30	652	taken	29	679
angry	30	653	weeks	29	680
cats	30	654	beautiful	28	681
glass	30	655	body	28	682
goal	30	656	enough	28	683
gun	30	657	except	28	684
high	30	658	exciting	28	685
loved	30	659	flat	28	686
part	30	660	ghosts	28	687
shed	30	661	hat	28	688
stood	30	662	hid	28	689
sunny	30	663	match	28	690
tired	29	664	moved	28	691
bell	29	665	nose	28	692
brothers	29	666	number	28	693
closed	29	667	sandwiches	28	694
coach	29	668	seven	28	695
doors	29	669	shopping	28	696
eating	29	670	sign	28	697
fair	29	671	ask	27	698
hill	29	672	bones	27	699
job	29	673	build	27	700

cross	27	701	fight	26	728
donkey	27	702	friendly	26	729
further	27	703	ice-cream	26	730
hungry	27	704	jolly	26	731
jump	27	705	ladies	26	732
lay	27	706	living	26	733
named	27	707	miles	26	734
rabbits	27	708	nest	26	735
roof	27	709	nobody	26	736
silver	27	710	poor	26	737
skin	27	711	post	26	738
sound	27	712	pot	26	739
takes	27	713	pretty	26	740
team	27	714	seaside	26	741
throw	27	715	short	26	742
toys	27	716	shut	26	743
treasure	27	717	soup	26	744
won't	27	718	spider	26	745
born	26	719	spinning-wheel	26	746
carpet	26	720	stand	26	747
chips	26	721	those	26	748
chocolate	26	722	Thursday	26	749
club	26	723	uncle	26	750
cousin	26	724	van	26	751
cried	26	725	waiting	26	752
dinosaur	26	726	wash	26	753
doctor	26	727	watching	26	754

wear	26	755	against	24	782
whale	26	756	became	24	783
bags	25	757	broken	24	784
blow	25	758	bubble	24	785
coat	25	759	captain	24	786
cousins	25	760	card	24	787
falling	25	761	care	24	788
helped	25	762	cottage	24	789
hunting	25	763	early	24	790
late	25	764	excited	24	791
library	25	765	gets	24	792
medicine	25	766	grew	24	793
mine	25	767	haunted	24	794
mountain	25	768	holidays	24	795
phone	25	769	horrible	24	796
pieces	25	770	houses	24	797
prince	25	771	line	24	798
princess	25	772	mole	24	799
sent	25	773	mouth	24	800
shops	25	774	mud	24	801
sick	25	775	onto	24	802
stones	25	776	seat	24	803
talk	25	777	she's	24	804
tied	25	778	slide	24	805
times	25	779	station	24	806
toy	25	780	surprise	24	807
village	25	781	trap	24	808

true	24	809		bears	22	836
without	24	810		bridge	22	837
already	23	811		busy	22	838
animal	23	812		cliff	22	839
arrived	23	813		crash	22	840
cage	23	814		earth	22	841
carried	23	815		enjoyed	22	842
carrots	23	816		fudge	22	843
colour	23	817		likes	22	844
computer	23	818		loud	22	845
fighting	23	819		magician	22	846
forgot	23	820		married	22	847
fruit	23	821		noticed	22	848
gives	23	822		potatoes	22	849
golden	23	823		pressed	22	850
nine	23	824		puppy	22	851
picture	23	825		quiet	22	852
places	23	826		reading	22	853
robber	23	827		rope	22	854
seals	23	828		rushed	22	855
sleeping	23	829		sisters	22	856
television	23	830		stuff	22	857
trying	23	831		sweet	22	858
wake	23	832		toad	22	859
worked	23	833		win	22	860
worm	23	834		windows	22	861
aeroplane	22	835		wolf	22	862

woman	22	863	bright	20	890
bat	21	864	cakes	20	891
bath	21	865	climb	20	892
bikes	21	866	cream	20	893
crab	21	867	dinosaurs	20	894
cry	21	868	dry	20	895
engine	21	869	ducks	20	896
growing	21	870	fluffy	20	897
gymnastics	21	871	glad	20	898
horses	21	872	herself	20	899
led	21	873	hotel	20	900
matter	21	874	lions	20	901
model	21	875	luckily	20	902
nuts	21	876	mad	20	903
parents	21	877	may	20	904
planet	21	878	no-one	20	905
rich	21	879	pack	20	906
robot	21	880	packed	20	907
rocket	21	881	parrot	20	908
rocks	21	882	pocket	20	909
spell	21	883	pull	20	910
tunnel	21	884	quick	20	911
wife	21	885	robbers	20	912
writing	21	886	size	20	913
attic	20	887	sort	20	914
bits	20	888	stars	20	915
boots	20	889	stepped	20	916

steps	20	917	pig	19	944
storm	20	918	playtime	19	945
tiny	20	919	queen	19	946
war	20	920	ring	19	947
wished	20	921	score	19	948
young	20	922	slowly	19	949
biggest	19	923	smell	19	950
bucket	19	924	snowman	19	951
chicken	19	925	spring	19	952
circus	19	926	strong	19	953
crocodile	19	927	sure	19	954
doesn't	19	928	talked	19	955
elephant	19	929	tall	19	956
else	19	930	tripped	19	957
fairies	19	931	Tuesday	19	958
farm	19	932	washing	19	959
free	19	933	wet	19	960
grabbed	19	934	wild	19	961
hide	19	935	write	19	962
knife	19	936	yet	19	963
knock	19	937	alien	18	964
lake	19	938	beside	18	965
laughed	19	939	bread	18	966
lucky	19	940	cannot	18	967
mind	19	941	chased	18	968
monkeys	19	942	clean	18	969
nan	19	943	eats	18	970

faster	18	971	babies	17	998
flash	18	972	bush	17	999
flower	18	973	chair	17	1000
lines	18	974	crisps	17	1001
owl	18	975	diamond	17	1002
passage	18	976	die	17	1003
pay	18	977	disappeared	17	1004
pop	18	978	drinks	17	1005
poured	18	979	eaten	17	1006
professor	18	980	eye	17	1007
send	18	981	film	17	1008
ships	18	982	following	17	1009
since	18	983	gran	17	1010
somebody	18	984	grandma	17	1011
swings	18	985	hands	17	1012
tank	18	986	heads	17	1013
tap	18	987	horn	17	1014
though	18	988	hut	17	1015
tomorrow	18	989	ill	17	1016
torch	18	990	keeper	17	1017
tower	18	991	knight	17	1018
twelve	18	992	laugh	17	1019
Wednesday	18	993	letters	17	1020
whistle	18	994	meet	17	1021
wooden	18	995	office	17	1022
able	17	996	ones	17	1023
airport	17	997	owner	17	1024

picnic	17	1025	fishing	16	1052
pictures	17	1026	friend's	16	1053
plants	17	1027	friendship	16	1054
rang	17	1028	frogs	16	1055
remembered	17	1029	fur	16	1056
rush	17	1030	golf	16	1057
save	17	1031	goodbye	16	1058
schoolgirls	17	1032	haven't	16	1059
suit	17	1033	invisible	16	1060
super	17	1034	journey	16	1061
taking	17	1035	jumping	16	1062
thin	17	1036	kick	16	1063
wondered	17	1037	kicked	16	1064
works	17	1038	kinds	16	1065
bank	16	1039	leaf	16	1066
bar	16	1040	listen	16	1067
between	16	1041	mean	16	1068
bowl	16	1042	moment	16	1069
caravan	16	1043	newspaper	16	1070
change	16	1044	palace	16	1071
climbing	16	1045	pencils	16	1072
coffee	16	1046	player	16	1073
covered	16	1047	pound	16	1074
creatures	16	1048	pushed	16	1075
eight	16	1049	riding	16	1076
explore	16	1050	rooster	16	1077
factory	16	1051	rose	16	1078

saved	16	1079	heart	15	1106
share	16	1080	igloo	15	1107
shouting	16	1081	jet	15	1108
snake	16	1082	nanny	15	1109
song	16	1083	naughty	15	1110
star	16	1084	net	15	1111
thinking	16	1085	news	15	1112
tiger	16	1086	normal	15	1113
trousers	16	1087	power	15	1114
twenty	16	1088	present	15	1115
ugly	16	1089	remember	15	1116
weather	16	1090	safe	15	1117
who's	16	1091	scream	15	1118
alive	15	1092	smaller	15	1119
anyone	15	1093	soft	15	1120
arms	15	1094	sports	15	1121
balloon	15	1095	standing	15	1122
biscuits	15	1096	sword	15	1123
carry	15	1097	trick	15	1124
crown	15	1098	trouble	15	1125
dance	15	1099	tunes	15	1126
doll	15	1100	wears	15	1127
drove	15	1101	weekend	15	1128
eagle	15	1102	wide	15	1129
feed	15	1103	wing	15	1130
fence	15	1104	wonderful	15	1131
forward	15	1105	apples	14	1132

bathroom	14	1133	managed	14	1160
belt	14	1134	mansion	14	1161
block	14	1135	maths	14	1162
bored	14	1136	older	14	1163
break	14	1137	pedal	14	1164
brother's	14	1138	plays	14	1165
case	14	1139	pm	14	1166
chairs	14	1140	policeman	14	1167
cheeky	14	1141	purple	14	1168
clouds	14	1142	raining	14	1169
cows	14	1143	rides	14	1170
dangerous	14	1144	says	14	1171
duck	14	1145	search	14	1172
enjoy	14	1146	servants	14	1173
feeling	14	1147	shark	14	1174
finally	14	1148	sharp	14	1175
fit	14	1149	sides	14	1176
garage	14	1150	sight	14	1177
gate	14	1151	singing	14	1178
happiness	14	1152	slept	14	1179
helps	14	1153	somewhere	14	1180
hippo	14	1154	songs	14	1181
jungle	14	1155	step	14	1182
killer	14	1156	stories	14	1183
ladder	14	1157	string	14	1184
large	14	1158	swans	14	1185
longer	14	1159	teachers	14	1186

theatre	14	1187	doctor's	13	1214
trapped	14	1188	ended	13	1215
underneath	14	1189	evil	13	1216
usually	14	1190	extinct	13	1217
washed	14	1191	famous	13	1218
we'll	14	1192	ferry	13	1219
wouldn't	14	1193	fired	13	1220
accident	13	1194	fortune	13	1221
answer	13	1195	guide	13	1222
base	13	1196	hallowe'en	13	1223
beaver	13	1197	hundred	13	1224
beginning	13	1198	hunter	13	1225
boxes	13	1199	jail	13	1226
building	13	1200	kit	13	1227
bye	13	1201	lift	13	1228
cards	13	1202	lifted	13	1229
caribou	13	1203	lump	13	1230
cart	13	1204	map	13	1231
choose	13	1205	metal	13	1232
church	13	1206	missed	13	1233
close	13	1207	notice	13	1234
cloud	13	1208	others	13	1235
cub	13	1209	pass	13	1236
deer	13	1210	phoned	13	1237
dig	13	1211	realized	13	1238
disco	13	1212	roar	13	1239
distance	13	1213	rockets	13	1240

rubbish	13	1241	badger	12	1268
screaming	13	1242	beds	12	1269
seemed	13	1243	bees	12	1270
slipped	13	1244	burnt	12	1271
smashed	13	1245	camping	12	1272
speed	13	1246	chase	12	1273
spend	13	1247	drank	12	1274
spirit	13	1248	dresses	12	1275
straw	13	1249	empty	12	1276
sudden	13	1250	eskimos	12	1277
swam	13	1251	feathers	12	1278
tadpoles	13	1252	final	12	1279
themselves	13	1253	future	12	1280
thunder	13	1254	goals	12	1281
tickets	13	1255	held	12	1282
tooth	13	1256	jelly	12	1283
tummy	13	1257	lamp	12	1284
wicked	13	1258	lead	12	1285
witch's	13	1259	leader	12	1286
words	13	1260	loads	12	1287
youngest	13	1261	midnight	12	1288
allowed	12	1262	months	12	1289
answered	12	1263	mountains	12	1290
anymore	12	1264	nan's	12	1291
anyway	12	1265	neck	12	1292
appeared	12	1266	noisy	12	1293
awake	12	1267	pair	12	1294

pen	12	1295	they're	12	1322
pencil	12	1296	track	12	1323
pipe	12	1297	wants	12	1324
plant	12	1298	wardrobe	12	1325
pub	12	1299	we're	12	1326
puts	12	1300	wore	12	1327
quarter	12	1301	aeroplanes	11	1328
racing	12	1302	army	11	1329
radio	12	1303	aunt	11	1330
rat	12	1304	auntie	11	1331
real	12	1305	band	11	1332
robots	12	1306	battle	11	1333
sailed	12	1307	beat	11	1334
sang	12	1308	bone	11	1335
shadow	12	1309	boring	11	1336
shout	12	1310	brain	11	1337
sister's	12	1311	bubbles	11	1338
sledge	12	1312	bull	11	1339
slow	12	1313	bushes	11	1340
snowball	12	1314	buttons	11	1341
son	12	1315	careful	11	1342
spots	12	1316	chance	11	1343
stream	12	1317	chest	11	1344
surprised	12	1318	chose	11	1345
tables	12	1319	coats	11	1346
teddy	12	1320	coins	11	1347
telling	12	1321	cook	11	1348

cooking	11	1349	laughing	11	1376
count	11	1350	luck	11	1377
crashed	11	1351	maggot	11	1378
creature	11	1352	market	11	1379
crept	11	1353	mice	11	1380
crossed	11	1354	mile	11	1381
crystal	11	1355	moving	11	1382
delicious	11	1356	note	11	1383
dragons	11	1357	patch	11	1384
drawing	11	1358	pence	11	1385
drive	11	1359	picking	11	1386
driver	11	1360	plan	11	1387
dug	11	1361	pleased	11	1388
Easter	11	1362	pointed	11	1389
eventually	11	1363	pole	11	1390
farmer	11	1364	pots	11	1391
fields	11	1365	pudding	11	1392
finding	11	1366	quintet	11	1393
finger	11	1367	record	11	1394
fingers	11	1368	roads	11	1395
flute	11	1369	rolled	11	1396
goodbye	11	1370	rough	11	1397
grown	11	1371	row	11	1398
hey	11	1372	rushing	11	1399
important	11	1373	sack	11	1400
insects	11	1374	shape	11	1401
kittens	11	1375	shapes	11	1402

sheep	11	1403		ambulance	10	1430
shoot	11	1404		art	10	1431
shoulder	11	1405		aunty	10	1432
sing	11	1406		autumn	10	1433
smoke	11	1407		bars	10	1434
spare	11	1408		beating	10	1435
spirits	11	1409		blot	10	1436
stickleback	11	1410		blows	10	1437
sticks	11	1411		board	10	1438
such	11	1412		boats	10	1439
tails	11	1413		boiled	10	1440
telephone	11	1414		breezes	10	1441
temple	11	1415		bumped	10	1442
toilet	11	1416		burrow	10	1443
trapdoor	11	1417		calm	10	1444
tricks	11	1418		canal	10	1445
turns	11	1419		cannon	10	1446
upset	11	1420		cardboard	10	1447
waves	11	1421		chasing	10	1448
wedding	11	1422		cheese	10	1449
women	11	1423		closer	10	1450
wonder	11	1424		coloured	10	1451
working	11	1425		court	10	1452
worry	11	1426		crabs	10	1453
wrote	11	1427		crack	10	1454
above	10	1428		decorations	10	1455
address	10	1429		desk	10	1456

detective	10	1457	lightning	10	1484
dirty	10	1458	lined	10	1485
dived	10	1459	listened	10	1486
dreaming	10	1460	litter	10	1487
driving	10	1461	load	10	1488
eskimo	10	1462	log	10	1489
especially	10	1463	mail	10	1490
evening	10	1464	mallards	10	1491
feast	10	1465	manager	10	1492
filled	10	1466	metres	10	1493
fix	10	1467	missing	10	1494
frozen	10	1468	muddy	10	1495
genie	10	1469	necklace	10	1496
group	10	1470	nests	10	1497
hanging	10	1471	nurse	10	1498
happen	10	1472	oak	10	1499
hate	10	1473	ourselves	10	1500
hay	10	1474	paid	10	1501
helicopter	10	1475	parcel	10	1502
hiding	10	1476	peas	10	1503
hurry	10	1477	penny	10	1504
isn't	10	1478	pets	10	1505
jar	10	1479	players	10	1506
jewels	10	1480	points	10	1507
kettle	10	1481	poison	10	1508
ladybird	10	1482	popped	10	1509
least	10	1483	postman	10	1510

powder	10	1511	triangles	10	1538
prison	10	1512	underground	10	1539
railway	10	1513	walls	10	1540
roll	10	1514	waterfall	10	1541
runs	10	1515	where's	10	1542
sail	10	1516	wishes	10	1543
sandy	10	1517	wizard	10	1544
scarf	10	1518	afterwards	9	1545
seeds	10	1519	age	9	1546
sell	10	1520	ahead	9	1547
shell	10	1521	almost	9	1548
shells	10	1522	apart	9	1549
shook	10	1523	assembly	9	1550
shorts	10	1524	attacked	9	1551
soil	10	1525	barn	9	1552
sounded	10	1526	beak	9	1553
spade	10	1527	bench	9	1554
splash	10	1528	boil	9	1555
stomach	10	1529	boo	9	1556
supper	10	1530	budgie	9	1557
taxi	10	1531	camp	9	1558
tells	10	1532	cheered	9	1559
third	10	1533	child	9	1560
tidy	10	1534	classes	9	1561
tigers	10	1535	clear	9	1562
tin	10	1536	container	9	1563
tipped	10	1537	corn	9	1564

cow	9	1565	invited	9	1592
crew	9	1566	judo	9	1593
cricket	9	1567	juice	9	1594
deck	9	1568	juicy	9	1595
desert	9	1569	jumpers	9	1596
double	9	1570	keys	9	1597
dust	9	1571	leading	9	1598
easy	9	1572	learn	9	1599
edge	9	1573	lesson	9	1600
elephants	9	1574	lets	9	1601
eleven	9	1575	lit	9	1602
escape	9	1576	local	9	1603
fed	9	1577	logs	9	1604
float	9	1578	meal	9	1605
follow	9	1579	moves	9	1606
footprints	9	1580	musical	9	1607
fright	9	1581	noises	9	1608
gates	9	1582	oil	9	1609
giving	9	1583	pantomime	9	1610
glue	9	1584	piano	9	1611
gnomes	9	1585	pit	9	1612
goose	9	1586	pitch	9	1613
guess	9	1587	poem	9	1614
helping	9	1588	poppy	9	1615
hen	9	1589	popular	9	1616
holding	9	1590	pretended	9	1617
huge	9	1591	prey	9	1618

putting	9	1619	we've	9	1646
rainbow	9	1620	wearing	9	1647
register	9	1621	you'll	9	1648
rid	9	1622	you've	9	1649
roast	9	1623	I'd	9	1650
sink	9	1624	afraid	8	1651
spear	9	1625	alarm	8	1652
spiders	9	1626	amazed	8	1653
spoke	9	1627	area	8	1654
spokes	9	1628	bananas	8	1655
spooky	9	1629	bats	8	1656
spoon	9	1630	bet	8	1657
spread	9	1631	biscuit	8	1658
squirrels	9	1632	bite	8	1659
steam	9	1633	blown	8	1660
stole	9	1634	bodies	8	1661
stove	9	1635	brilliant	8	1662
struck	9	1636	bump	8	1663
swan	9	1637	cabin	8	1664
swing	9	1638	cafe	8	1665
throwing	9	1639	calling	8	1666
tonight	9	1640	carved	8	1667
tool	9	1641	chick	8	1668
touched	9	1642	chief	8	1669
traffic	9	1643	chimney	8	1670
unhappy	9	1644	coal	8	1671
wand	9	1645	colourful	8	1672

control	8	1673	heath	8	1700
counted	8	1674	hidden	8	1701
cracked	8	1675	hippopotamus	8	1702
dare	8	1676	hunt	8	1703
deeper	8	1677	join	8	1704
disguise	8	1678	jumper	8	1705
fainted	8	1679	kite	8	1706
fairyland	8	1680	lane	8	1707
feeding	8	1681	leaving	8	1708
figure	8	1682	lie	8	1709
fixed	8	1683	loving	8	1710
flames	8	1684	lying	8	1711
flashes	8	1685	main	8	1712
floated	8	1686	mat	8	1713
floating	8	1687	meant	8	1714
flyer	8	1688	meanwhile	8	1715
forever	8	1689	mop	8	1716
forget	8	1690	mostly	8	1717
fresh	8	1691	museum	8	1718
geranium	8	1692	nanna's	8	1719
guard	8	1693	nasty	8	1720
gum	8	1694	needed	8	1721
handball	8	1695	object	8	1722
hardly	8	1696	overboard	8	1723
hare	8	1697	paint	8	1724
harpoon	8	1698	pan	8	1725
heat	8	1699	pebbles	8	1726

peeped	8	1727	switch	8	1754
pillow	8	1728	teacher's	8	1755
planes	8	1729	tennis	8	1756
polar	8	1730	test	8	1757
pools	8	1731	thanks	8	1758
porridge	8	1732	ticket	8	1759
potato	8	1733	tide	8	1760
pouring	8	1734	toilets	8	1761
prize	8	1735	tracks	8	1762
push	8	1736	understand	8	1763
rode	8	1737	upside	8	1764
rooms	8	1738	ways	8	1765
rubbed	8	1739	whenever	8	1766
scary	8	1740	word	8	1767
seconds	8	1741	worms	8	1768
shore	8	1742	worried	8	1769
shrinking	8	1743	adventures	7	1770
sir	8	1744	aid	7	1771
skate	8	1745	alone	7	1772
skipping	8	1746	arrow	7	1773
smells	8	1747	attack	7	1774
socks	8	1748	badge	7	1775
speak	8	1749	badly	7	1776
squid	8	1750	balls	7	1777
staying	8	1751	banged	7	1778
stepmother	8	1752	basket	7	1779
submarine	8	1753	baths	7	1780

bedtime	7	1781	collywobbles	7	1808
binoculars	7	1782	competition	7	1809
bomb	7	1783	cooked	7	1810
bonfire	7	1784	corners	7	1811
breath	7	1785	corridor	7	1812
breathe	7	1786	cot	7	1813
brick	7	1787	crawled	7	1814
broomstick	7	1788	creepy	7	1815
burgled	7	1789	cubs	7	1816
buried	7	1790	danger	7	1817
capsized	7	1791	date	7	1818
Care-bears	7	1792	den	7	1819
caring	7	1793	dormitory	7	1820
carnival	7	1794	drinking	7	1821
catching	7	1795	drum	7	1822
chains	7	1796	drunk	7	1823
chicks	7	1797	ear	7	1824
children's	7	1798	easily	7	1825
chopped	7	1799	eater	7	1826
circle	7	1800	either	7	1827
clarinet	7	1801	extra	7	1828
claws	7	1802	faces	7	1829
cleaned	7	1803	fallen	7	1830
cleaning	7	1804	fantastic	7	1831
cloak	7	1805	Father-Christmas	7	1832
clown	7	1806	fête	7	1833
cola	7	1807	fir	7	1834

flag	7	1835	meeting	7	1862
flood	7	1836	mess	7	1863
given	7	1837	million	7	1864
hadn't	7	1838	mission	7	1865
harbour	7	1839	monsters	7	1866
heavy	7	1840	motor	7	1867
hide-and-seek	7	1841	nail	7	1868
holes	7	1842	nights	7	1869
homes	7	1843	none	7	1870
homework	7	1844	offshore	7	1871
horns	7	1845	operation	7	1872
human	7	1846	ordinary	7	1873
indoors	7	1847	packet	7	1874
jealous	7	1848	panda	7	1875
judge	7	1849	parts	7	1876
knowing	7	1850	patterns	7	1877
laid	7	1851	peach	7	1878
landing	7	1852	penalty	7	1879
lazy	7	1853	piccolo	7	1880
lemonade	7	1854	pigeon	7	1881
lighthouse	7	1855	point	7	1882
liquid	7	1856	potion	7	1883
lock	7	1857	programme	7	1884
lolly	7	1858	questions	7	1885
lonely	7	1859	races	7	1886
master	7	1860	rather	7	1887
meadow	7	1861	reached	7	1888

restaurant	7	1889	stall	7	1917
rhino	7	1890	stroke	7	1918
roses	7	1891	support	7	1919
sailing	7	1892	surface	7	1920
salad	7	1893	tasted ˙	7	1921
salt	7	1894	tents	7	1922
schools	7	1895	terrible	7	1923
seem	7	1896	touch	7	1924
servant	7	1897	towel	7	1925
shaking	7	1898	travelled	7	1926
sheepdogs	7	1899	tripping	7	1927
shelf	7	1900	twice	7	1928
shining	7	1901	video	7	1929
sits	7	1902	volcano	7	1930
skins	7	1903	walks	7	1931
skirt	7	1904	waved	7	1932
skirts	7	1905	whatever	7	1933
sledges	7	1906	wheels	7	1934
slip	7	1907	wire	7	1935
smallest	7	1908	wobbly	7	1936
snooker	7	1909	woken	7	1937
sometime	7	1910	wondering	7	1938
sore	7	1911	yelled	7	1939
sorts	7	1912	yours	7	1940
spacecraft	7	1913	altogether	6	1941
sparkling	7	1914	angle	6	1942
spine	7	1915	armour	6	1943
spotted	7	1916	auntie's	6	1944

awful	6	1945		coconuts	6	1973
badges	6	1946		collected	6	1974
banana	6	1947		cool	6	1975
become	6	1948		costumes	6	1976
bee	6	1949		cover	6	1977
beer	6	1950		crackling	6	1978
believed	6	1951		curtains	6	1979
below	6	1952		cushions	6	1980
bin	6	1953		danced	6	1981
blizzard	6	1954		death	6	1982
boards	6	1955		dinners	6	1983
boom	6	1956		discovered	6	1984
bowls	6	1957		dishes	6	1985
branch	6	1958		doctors	6	1986
branches	6	1959		dolls	6	1987
bristle	6	1960		draw	6	1988
brush	6	1961		drew	6	1989
buildings	6	1962		drip	6	1990
bunny	6	1963		drowned	6	1991
burn	6	1964		dull	6	1992
buzz	6	1965		dusty	6	1993
canary	6	1966		entrance	6	1994
candy	6	1967		escaped	6	1995
cargo	6	1968		fall	6	1996
carrying	6	1969		feather	6	1997
chickens	6	1970		fellow	6	1998
chop	6	1971		fierce	6	1999
clever	6	1972		fifteen	6	2000

Observations and Comparisons from the Research Team

As the most recent previous vocabulary research undertaken in this country was by Edwards and Gibbon in 1964, some comparison between that research and the present research results seemed an interesting line of enquiry. The following comparisons have been made between the LDA 7-year old's Word List and the Edwards and Gibbon 7-year old's Word List.

A comparison between LDA's top 100 words and the top 100 Edwards and Gibbon words (Words Your Children Use, 1964).

1   Words on LDA top 100 not appearing on Edwards and Gibbon top 100.

Word	Rank on LDA	Rank on E & G
into	58	106
would	67	179
their	69	110
could	73	145
do	76	107
what	78	153
as	79	124
off	81	103
people	83	122
if	89	133
door	90	187
ran	91	212
no	92	188
next	93	147
took	94	174
good	95	159
about	97	125

There are only 17 differences between the two top 100 words and the first 57 words on the LDA list are all on the Edwards and Gibbon list.

2   Words on Edwards and Gibbon top 100 not appearing on LDA top 100.

Word	Rank on LDA	Rank on E & G	Frequency on LDA
play	133	18	111
am	122	28	100
this	109	40	124
last	312	54	35
girl	114	56	110
mother	250	66	45
boy	107	70	129
lie	277	72	40
take	163	78	74
today	377	81	29
walk	131	82	91
too	128	83	97
tree	101	93	136
watch	488	94	22
car	150	95	79
from	105	97	133
yesterday	335	100	33

3   In a comparison with "carrier" words (i.e., those parts of speech which "carry along" the main nouns, verbs, adjectives and adverbs, i.e., pronouns, prepositions, conjunctions, auxilary verbs etc.) there were only nine differences between LDA and Edwards and Gibbon in the top 96 entries.

Of those words: —

(a) 'am' came 29th in E & G's list and only 122nd in LDA's list.

(b) The following were all ranked between 37 and 96 on E & G's list:

LDA ranking	LDA frequency	E & G
130	91	by
312	35	last
175	69	look
147	80	make
350	31	new
165	73	three
128	97	too
144	82	want

4   When considering the comparison between nouns, 55 were in the first 100 in the LDA Word List and both Edwards and Gibbon Word List.

The first ten nouns from each list occurred in the following order: —

LDA	E & G
day	day
home	home
mum	daddy
man	house
time	night
house	mummy
dad	girl
bed	man
dog	time
people	mother

Interestingly, the word 'school' ranked 11th in both lists.

Both lists had the following words in their top 100.

car	father	father
toys	dog	money
wood	brother	garden
story	room	food
name	rabbit	boy
birthday	tree	morning
sea	fire	flower
children	wood	sun
cat	road	dinner
sister	friend	shop
boat	baby	castle
witch	park	night
bed	door	water
tea	girl	bird
window	hair	game

5   The following words appeared on Edwards and Gibbon's vocabulary list in the top 100 nouns but *not* on LDA's top 100 nouns.

LDA ranking	LDA frequency	E & G
333	33	police
355	30	book
459	23	horse
478	22	party
508	21	train
512	20	bus
562	18	doll
752	13	seaside
865	11	television*
933	9	circus
1080	8	*TV
—	—	Cowboy

Top 100 nouns in LDA 7-year old's list

1	day	35	Christmas	69	father
2	home	36	witch	70	road
3	mum	37	story	71	woods
4	man	38	castle	72	forest
5	time	39	food	73	pool
6	house	40	park	74	sky
7	dad	41	giant	75	snow
8	bed	42	room	76	cup
9	dog	43	sister	77	moon
10	people	44	brother	78	paper
11	school	45	cave	79	sun
12	door	46	trees	80	bedroom
13	night	47	baby	81	snooker
14	name	48	boat	82	years
15	tree	49	wood	83	birthday
16	boy	50	daddy	84	ground
17	girl	51	lady	85	holiday
18	morning	52	men	86	wheel
19	water	53	snowman	87	toys
20	cat	54	wind	88	air
21	dragon	55	dinner	89	animals
22	mummy	56	clothes	90	game
23	friend	57	football	91	nose
24	children	58	sunflower	92	treasures
25	tea	59	bird	93	flowers
26	car	60	head	94	grass
27	king	61	sea	95	police
28	fire	62	hole	96	ghost
29	garden	63	mother	97	rabbit
30	friends	64	fish	98	bag
31	hair	65	zoo	99	boys
32	eyes	66	money	100	girls
33	shop	67	window		
34	balloon	68	beanstalk		

An Analysis of the top 100 nouns in the 7-year old's list

(i) 'family' words in top 100

home	mum	house	dad	bed	dog
boy	girl	cat	mummy	friend	children
tea	car	garden	friends	food	room
sister	brother	baby	daddy	dinner	mother
father	bedroom	toys	boys	girls	

(ii) 'story' words in top 100

dragon	witch	king	beanstalk	forest
castle	giant	cave	treasures	ghost

The word 'story' was used 63 times.

(iii) '1980's' words in research

Word	Frequency
video	3
computer	10
disco	12
devil	16
dinosaurs	23
monster	30
snooker	38

(none of these occur in Edwards and Gibbon's List of 1964)

(iv) Evidence of violence?

Word	Frequency	LDA ranking
dead	27	392
killed	26	417
died	23	453
die	13	725
dies	3	1879

'die', 'dead' and 'kill' were all ranked in the range 250-500 in the Edwards and Gibbon List.

(v) cowboy does not appear in the LDA list and it occurs in the range 0-250 in Edwards and Gibbon.

(vi) In LDA the word 'look' ranks 175 (89 in E & G); and the word 'here' ranks 167 (150 in E & G). It is interesting to note that these are key words in early reading scheme books, but do not appear to be so popular when children come to choose words for writing.

Top 100 nouns in LDA 8-year old's list

1	day	35	gold	69	land		
2	mum	36	sea	70	men		
3	home	37	window	71	noise		
4	time	38	Christmas	72	world		
5	house	39	shop	73	air		
6	people	40	sleep	74	bedroom		
7	dad	41	dragon	75	bird		
8	school	42	work	76	giant		
9	man	43	mummy	77	police		
10	bed	44	class	78	face		
11	door	45	fish	79	forest		
12	night	46	baby	80	table		
13	water	47	hole	81	ship		
14	morning	48	cave	82	birds		
15	name	49	head	83	person		
16	room	50	money	84	egg		
17	friends	51	trees	85	grass		
18	car	52	witch	86	sky		
19	friend	53	eyes	87	sweets		
20	tree	54	football	88	woods		
21	ghost	55	park	89	breakfast		
22	food	56	family	90	father		
23	dog	57	ball	91	train		
24	girl	58	birthday	92	place		
25	boy	59	box	93	spare		
26	wood	60	lady	94	Saturday		
27	tea	61	mother	95	snow		
28	fire	62	years	96	week		
29	children	63	hair	97	wind		
30	dinner	64	rabbit	98	castle		
31	brother	65	lunch	99	game		
32	cat	66	book	100	rain		
33	sister	67	road				
34	garden	68	days				

An analysis of top 100 nouns in the 8-year old's list

(i)   'family' words in top 100

mum	home	house	people	dad
school	man	bed	door	morning
friends	car	friend	tree	food
dog	girl	boy	tea	children
dinner	brother	cat	sister	garden
window	shop	sleep	mummy	class
baby	trees	family	mother	lunch
bedroom	breakfast	father		

(ii)   'story' words in top 100

ghost	gold	dragon	cave
giant	forest	castle	witch

(iii) "1980's" words in 8-year old's list

Word	Frequency
video	7
snooker	7
disco	13
computer	23
robots	12
robot	21
television	23
TV	33
BMX	13
dinosaurs	20
dinosaur	26

(iv)   Evidence of violence?

Word	Frequency
death	6
fighting	23
killed	39
kill	43
dead	49
died	73

A comparison of the top 10 nouns in the of 7-year old's list

7's	8's
day	day
home	mum
mum	home
man	time
time	house
house	people
dad	dad
bed	school
dog	man
people	bed

The only difference between the lists is that 7's have the word 'dog' (ranked 9th) whereas in the 8's list this word ranks 23rd, and 8's have the word 'school' (ranked 8th) whereas 7's have this word ranked 11th.

Nouns in 7-year old's top 100 not appearing in 8-year old's top 100

Word	Ranking	Word	Ranking	Word	Ranking
zoo	102	story	120	nose	237
boat	103	holiday	124	toys	247
wheel	104	king	126	snowman	357
animals	105	boys	131	balloon	419
daddy	107	clothes	133	snooker	842
paper	110	girls	142	beanstalk	—
bag	111	moon	166	ground	—
cup	117	pool	182	sunflower	—
flowers	118	sun	183	treasures	—

(The figures refer to the noun ranking order that these words appear on the 8's list.)

Thus, all but four words in the 7's top 100 are ranked on the 8's list.

73% of the nouns are common to both lists in the top 100.

Words on 8-year old's noun list not appearing on 7-year old's top 100.

gold	days	egg
sleep	land	sweets
work	noise	breakfast
class	world	train
family	face	place
ball	table	space
box	ship	Saturday
lunch	birds	week
book	person	rain

In the 7's list if the entries for 'mum' (279), 'mummy' (83) and 'mother' (45) are combined, the total frequency is 407 which makes it the second highest noun in frequency after the word 'day' (489). If 'mum's' is included the frequency is 416.

A similar totalling of entries for 8 achieves the frequency 910 which similarly makes it the second highest noun in frequency after the word 'day' (929). However, if 'mum's' is included in the total, then the frequency is 945 which makes it the most popular noun.

In both lists the most popular form was 'mum' followed by 'mummy', followed by 'mother'.

In the 7's list, if the entries for 'dad', 'daddy' and 'father' are combined the frequency is 296 which makes it the third most popular noun after 'day' (489) and 'home' (349). If 'dad's' is included, this brings the total to 310 and the ranking is not affected.

In the 8's list, the total frequency for 'dad' (379), 'father' (65) and 'daddy' (59) is 503 which makes it the fourth most used noun after 'day' (929), 'mum' (718) and 'home' (680). The inclusion of 'dad's' (29) does not affect this ranking.

Comments from the Research Team

1   A priority of this research has been to accurately represent the actual vocabulary children have used. However, when listing the nouns it is difficult to be sure whether a child has actually used that word as a noun or not. Some are easier than others to judge, e.g., whilst 'treasure' is more likely to be a noun rather than a verb, and 'chips' is probably being used as a noun, it is much more difficult to decide whether 'flat' is an adjective or a noun. In these instances the researcher's own intuition has been used. Consequently, words such as 'name' or 'water' which rank high on the vocabulary lists incorporate both the noun and verb usage and this naturally influences their position in the ranking order.

2   No distinction has been made between one child using a word many times and many children using a word once.

3   Proper names (with a few exceptions such as 'Christmas') have not been listed.

4   Plurals of nouns have been listed separately.

5   Comparative and superlative forms have been listed separately.

6   All verb forms are shown separately, e.g., 'walk', 'walks', 'walking', 'walked'.

7   Possessives are listed separately, e.g., 'teacher', 'teacher's'.

Inevitably such a survey reveals the diversity of ability in children of this age, but the overriding factor to emerge from the analysis is that children have a story they want to tell and, although some may have greater skill in the presentation of their writing, the vast majority of children understand the concept of story and are able to communicate this in their writing.

Bibliography

Arvidson G. L. NZCER Alphabetical Spelling Lists, Wellington, New Zealand. Council for Educational Research, 1960.

Burroughs G.E.R. A Study of the Vocabulary of Young Children. University of Birmingham 1957. Oliver and Boyd.

Edwards R.P.A. & Gibbon V. Words Your Children Use, An Infant Vocabulary Survey. Burke 1964.

Fry E. The New Infant Word List. The Reading Teacher. December 1980.

Horn E. A Basic Writing Vocabulary. 10,000 words commonly used in Writing. Monographs in Education, First Series, No. 4, State University of Iowa, 1926.

Schonell F.J. The Essential Spelling List. 3,200 Everyday Words. Macmillan Education 1932.

Thorndike E.L. The Teacher's Word Book of 10,000 Words. New York: Teachers College, Columbia University 1921.

Thorndike E.L. The Teacher's Word Book of 30,000 Words. New York: Teachers College, Columbia University 1944.